The Flowers
of
Nonchalance

Kallisto Gaia Press Inc.
1801 E. 51st Street
Suite 365-246
Austin TX 78723
info@kallistogaiapress.org
(254) 654-7205

Cover Design: Tony Burnett
Edited by: Tate Lewis-Carroll

ISBN: 978-1-*952224-28-7

Table of Contents

The Flowers of Nonchalance

poems

Dan Smart

To Mike, for seeing what was there.

Before one studies Zen, mountains are mountains and waters are waters; after a first glimpse into the truth of Zen, mountains are no longer mountains and waters are no longer waters; after enlightenment, mountains are once again mountains and waters once again waters.

—Dōgen

HOW TO SING

All the weakest sounds
of things—

faint sizzle
of a dwindled candle,

subtle breathing of the newborn
leaves,

tarnished old bell
feebly repeating
the only note it knows—

listen
unceasingly—everything
teaches.

GRADUAL

Whether or not you are
there to notice, first
thing in the morning
there is mist—

low on cold hills
always somewhere in the distance
outside your door
in between the city you live in
and the rest of the world
which purportedly exists

blue as the first church bells'
dull round ringing
still lying heavy in its furrowed beds
shrouded by mazes
of dark woods, and dreaming—

just as you were a minute ago—
of being

touched by warm light
made gradually
unafraid, and rising

one more time
to become the entire air.

MORNING ROUTINE

Before dawn each day—
impossibly
high, impossibly far away

uncountable
savage blast furnaces
fire

just to power
the weak light
that yawns through

the kitchen window
by which you like
to sit and sip tea

and thumb through a few
pages of Marlowe,
or maybe

sketch a fragment
of your own about
cornflowers—

before the slightest flutter
of one lid
of one eye

pitiless factories,
galactic in size: all working
triple-overtime

toward an infinite quota—
completely for free—
just to manufacture

those sanitized
unbreakable
I-beams of time

which later you
will blithely call
small hours.

THE VANITY

It's no contest—every morning, light
fills this room much better
than I do,

makes even the cold tile
patterns look more
familiar

than that copy of me who
slowly enters, avarice
still numbed;

who always woozily refuses
to be the container,
even as

he grows larger, sharper-
cornered, and more
vacant—until,

slightly confused, he'll start to pull
back a little from
the mirror.

Still, he usually does not look
quite as shocked as I
think he ought to.

MERWIN IN THE KITCHEN

For better—and, of course,
for worse—when I pick up one
of your smart slender books,

it puts a sort of simple frame
made of un-lacquered wood
around the minutia of morning.

It is—you'd be relieved
to hear, I think—a subtle feeling:
like gravity,

like insects' wings beating
from way out there on the fringe
of your garden;

I find myself
pausing between pages—
to trace with a finger

a certain pattern in the
grain of the table,
to listen more closely

to the sonata
of the fridge compressor,
to gently swirl

this glass of cool milk—
allowing it
to dawn on me

(the way dawn itself must
dawn every day at the end
of a rainy Maui night)

 that I wouldn't enjoy it
if I drank it too quickly,
that any second—

this one—or maybe
the one that comes next—
could be

an equator,
some invisible
but significant

prime meridian,
the exact dead
center of my life.

AT THE CROSSWALK

In the milky sky above the square,
the familiar almost-equilibrium
of pigeons

having burst from their fountain
at the gunning
of green light engines

now tickling the low clouds
in undulating ripples,
diving and swooping in hapless formation—

making me
feel restless; making me feel
small.

For a moment, I suppose
I would like to be
one of them—

but no, that's not
quite right, is it?
I'd like to be them all.

THE IMMORTAL MADE SIMPLE

Try this—
place a smart little
gift shop bouquet

of red local flowers
on the table
near the window

in their
hospital room
at the right time of day—

then watch
for a minute (though they
aren't yet awake)

the auroras cascade:
the amaranthine import
of Loveliness itself

as it floods in
to drench the tedious
and inconsequential—

the antiseptic gray
space in which
Commonplace must exist;

and then
come home and tell me
you still don't know

what forever
is, or today
was for.

*FOOTNOTE TO FROST

Nothing gold can
stay, he wrote,

but nothing
turned precious
overnight, either.

Treasure is so
because, first,
it's been lost;

and that need
burns worst which
takes longest

to arrive.
Like diamond
from coal,

the obstruction
tends the goal—

the mind
must be squeezed

til it caves
into a soul.

FORGERY

Apropos
of the cold, blank
absurdity of the cosmos,

the iron
in a blast furnace
gets hotter than the fire;

a few fragmentary lines,
inscribed after
the fact,

may come, with time,
to mean

more than the entire
experience.

INVINCIBILITY POEM

Listen—even this
is a distraction; words,

like hailstones
disturbing the surface

of a deep and melancholy ocean.
It's only when

every sound, inside and out,
finally stops—that you can hear

the song of grace—
the source of the huge, cold waves,

the faintest music of
the planet smoothly turning—

its only lyric—
unsung, unheard, transmitted only

as a pattern of undulating insight—
an impassable question:

what is the real shape
of your face?

Look at me
talk to you
without even
having to

tap a clammy
tongue against
the backs
of my teeth: hot stuff,

and heavy
too, if you
ask me—it's like
language

is a time machine
built out of
a DeLorean—
and then

some skinny
poem climbs inside
that loud suit
of armor—and drives.

VESSEL

A short poem
is not something
anyone owns;

it's more like
the decorative box
it might come in.

If you want, you can
put something in it
that you love—

or perhaps
feel anxious about
finally being rid of—

then step back,
maybe snap
a quick photograph,

just to see
how it looks.

BYPRODUCT

There are mornings
when the very first thing

is the need
to have an idea.

And then,
there are evenings
where the last idea standing

is the desperate
need to fall
asleep.

*

I think I need
to clear my head.

I think I'm becoming
too interested

in the way
being interested
generates fumes

we call "finitude,"
which must then be
exhausted.

*

How is it
each day

feels so far away
from the last

when really there's just
that tepid, thin stream

of tedious dreams
to recap in-between?

THE PRICE

It's a beautiful thing I suppose at
first, outside my window

each morning—a hundred or so
sparrows that can't resist singing,

each punching a hole in
the cheap silence, sharpening

to a nice fine point
another one of the universe's

amorphous lumps of potentiality,
spinning one more dull strand

of space—formerly reserved
for something tedious

to occur—into the gold
of what's actually happening

even as I bend
to write it.

But I admire them less
when I descend to street level.

Walking past their lean environs,
it isn't difficult to see

that the price they pay
for their kinetic abilities—

their singing prowess, their
admirable near-weightlessness,

their sleek fleetness of wing
and of foot in the lilac bushes—

is instant panic
at the slightest hint of foot traffic

and an unwinnable war
for territory and resources

against even the least
formidable wind.

20

AUTHORIAL INTENT

Who's to say, truly,
what you should
or shouldn't do?

Wait just a minute;
before you give your answer,

stand up and fashion
a small cup
from your words—

then brew
a little bit
of hot coffee up

and pour it straight in there,
with all the rough certitude

of an omniscient,
omnipotent,
omnibenevolent narrator,

taking careful notice
of what happens
to your shoes.

Now: tell
your audience—
who makes the rules?

AN ABSENCE OF COOPERATION

What's the difference between
the silence
of the tiger

lily and
the tiger sleeping—
between the pale lotus

flower and the still-paler
moon smeared loosely on the
surrounding water?

Even closer
to home, I hear so many
of these absences

which seem to work together—
the quiet of morning
coffee in my cup

and of the downstairs
neighbors who
moved out last month;

the peace of the municipal vehicle
at the end of the cul-de-sac
not backing up

and the similar tranquility
of the steeple bell around the corner
during all the minutes

that mercifully exist
in between those horribly
ironclad hours.

In fact, there must be hundreds
of thousands of different
kinds of silence,

each with its own
loud dark way of knowing
something connected

to something else.
And I can't help but wonder—
which pair is the most like us?

I don't mean the species—I mean you
and me: two points,
two dots

at the top
of two necks, always connected,
always yolked as efficiently as possible

on the geodesic
surface of this planet, but never
really talking.

ALL THINGS

Late in October,
all things pursue ease.
Tinged

yellowish, moldy,
and brittle—all matter,
all space making peace.

All of us, too
are seeking release;
all at once,

our eyes,
knees, and speech
all go weak.

What we loved most—
what we sought
(so we thought)

from the world
more than pleasure
or experience—

was security:
a clean embrace, order
in the storm, shelter

from the subsequent
wreck. But now,
we haven't got

the spirit left
to wonder:
what sort of terrible

miracle comes next?
What summer child
could be born

of this marriage
between solemnity
and death?

25

CLOTHESLINE METAPHOR

A poem is a clothesline—
full of words washed clean

and hung up to dry
in the cool breeze

of forgetful eternities
and the antibacterial

gaze of virgin sun—
clean of those old usages

circulating for years,
clean of the stains

of school and work
and church—

exotic and bohemian sizes
billowing back and forth

of familiarly styled signifiers,
some nearly shapeless

from the stretching
of centuries, others bearing tags

as if never even worn before—
and some invisible

thread of love, spiked
here and there

with the stiff pins of longing,
holding the whole

gently swaying
apparatus together—an eerie curiosity

to find while walking
past a haunted house's backyard.

ACCUMULATION

With each passing week
of winter, it gets harder
to live with, harder
to live without

waking before seven
to find once again
the primly
coated neighborhood—

white
branches and cable wires,
all the status-
symbols and the beater cars

equalized.
As if
everything that was
last night has been

killed. And then raised up
one level of attainment—
younger,
but more wizened;

lighter, but increasingly
solid as carbon;
faster and looser, yet
ever more devoted

to its rigid discipline:
evincing a razor-
sharp purpose
in this imprecision.

THE TITLE COMES LAST

As if we're never quite sure
what we're asking for—
until some much more scientific
future version of ourselves
deigns to reanimate
the words we interred
a long time ago
in a galaxy far far away—
the title of a thing
almost always comes last.
If at first, this order of events
might seem counterintuitive,
the reality is, composition
can only proceed this way, since
the context of our intention
so often shifts as we
invent it—the only constant being
the implausibility
of discovery: tectonic plates hidden
beneath the feet of mountains,
asleep under oceans
of green liquid methane,
on the dimly lit fifth moon
of a strange exoplanet,
which has not even been looked at
by the eyes of sentient
beings yet, let alone colonized
and named.

RECIPE FOR DISASTER

Syllable
by syllable, the dead
become our words.

And our words,
in the right
environment, might

ferment
into our wishes.

And after millennia
of compounding
and sweetening underground,

some wishes are enriched
and condensed
to pure insight.

Meanwhile, the living
are wandering
and starving—

oblivious to the nourishment
extractable
from tragedy;

they'd rather live
on rancid fumes

from breathless
tales of loaves
and fishes.

PASTICHE

Strange to say,
but the mind
was made

to follow,
not to lead—

its Alice in gingham,
raked along
by the breeze,

not the rabbit
who torpedoes
fleet

and naked
through the field.

And you say strange
as if surprised,

as if mind itself
had been first
to suggest this,

but the fact is:
mind is clever
just

as a child is—
it can teach you
new dance steps

when it watches
then burlesques,

and it speaks to you
only in the most faultless
sentences,

to which it first listens,
then repeats.

DEADWEIGHT

Once in a while,
I try to imagine
a perfect spring day—

much like today—
when I am no longer
alive to record it:

the adolescent sun
and the vigorous wind,

the transcendental mix
of clouds and
boundless light—

and then, there's
the kid

racing with zeal
through a field
of matted grass,

his face knotted up
in a smirk of delight,

holding, with all
his might, to the string
of a kite.

But it's no use;
the harder I try
to picture it, the worse

it seems to get.
For starters, the kite

isn't really a kite;
instead, it's a bird.

And the kid
is not delighted;
his face is all grimace,

and he's running
for his life—as if he's
being forced,

during the eye
of some terrible storm,

to run for his life
and hold tight to my
burden.

WHAT'S ONE MORE

Outside my window, a lone crow's
desiccated
rasp of a caw,

first of autumn—like
bugle Taps
for the bygone season,

like a callus
that's thickening.

Well, what's one
more, I guess,

in the grand
scheme of this jointly tender
and excoriating world—

or do I mean,
one less?

SPOILS

Consider
the grimness
of the situation—

no word ever
wants
to be written.

Every hellish
minute at your
computer

is a clammy net
thrust into
roiling waters,

each sentence,
a pitiful
pittance of wealth—

a haul
of foul scraps, and sometimes
two wriggling fish

who'd much sooner
take their grim
chance in the depths

than suffocate here
in the name
of a hunger

you just could
no longer keep
to yourself.

NEW YEAR'S EVE

Already, I see it's getting late.
Soon, I must head out
to rake and gather

all that I've done
and failed to do
together;

and, without separating
one from the other,

to set fire to the bunch—
hear the words pop,
watch the deeds crackle.

For only then can I resume
my odd processes

of writing notes to myself
and making friends
idle promises

in the purified, ashen, desolate space
which another winter's
conflagration opens up.

ALONE

It's the brain,
locked away in silence
inside of its case,

that causes the moon
to appear

larger
on the horizon—

in order, perhaps,
to make itself
less conspicuous

to silence's stare,

and its distance,

and its dark.

*

It's the way,
when a body stops

for more than
one second,

this slithery sense
of permanence attaches—

the pit in your
stomach, say; or

a neutron star
far away.

*

I feel so alone.

Remind me again
what kind of stuff

we're all
made of—

bone meal and
table sugar,

or stardust
and wave functions,

or diploid cells,
cloned

and then cloned
and then

cloned?

LENT

In mid-March, after
turgid winter
loses its grip,

but the land is still
toothless

and stubborn
and dead,

the small flame
of a cardinal—all arrow-
sharp angles

of fierce red
and yellow—may look
more than a little

absurd
from your window.

But more perplexing still
to your groggy,
undead soul

are his fervid responsorial
and its notes
of braggadocio.

What earthly utility
could exist? you might wonder,

in his crowing like this
so early in the morning

about some new-
paradigm truth
long in coming,

the nature of which
only he was
made to know?

LE MOT JUSTE

Sometimes, I wish I was brave
as these crocus buds not yet waving,
for whom silence is eternity
and everything began yesterday;

instead, I cling to a stubborn faith
in an ancient language
which still can't convey
the religiousness of plain light.

But then, I don't know, I want to say,
somehow, maybe—
a decision you can't make
is one that's already been decided—

like the way the fragile skies
and ladies in gray keep weeping
and weeping each spring, but Jesus
keeps getting crucified anyway.

ACQUIESCENCE

After decades spent
avoiding the smallest
threat of inconvenience

posed by rich mythologies
that don't explain
a thing—at least,

not nearly as well
as they tend
to illuminate

the dry bones
and land mines which lie
in the brambles

and the cold
distant sun at the heart
of their explainer—

it seems you've grown more lenient;
you're now ready
to concede

that there's dignity
in the tyrannized,
in the role of doleful entertainer,

and most of all,
in the drudgery
of rolling up your sleeves

to pitch them
the salvation
of which you alone were told

but now are
far too old
to receive.

43

Over time, every
one
must collapse.

One
yields gradual, as if by many
serene degrees.

Another
does not; always hard to the
touch, it

just rots. But
time itself
glows unremittingly

green—
a tear-shaped
lump

that will not
ever
just relax.

WHAT HAPPENED

God, we are all such assholes—
every one of us, so greedy
for plot lines and the nine o'clock
news of our lives—so eager

to keep making
new things occur—

just so that we might
wear their learned lessons
sequentially stitched
across our bodies in public,

like keen-eyed little cub scouts
obsessed with earning badges.

But how often
do we ever
walk up to another in our tribe
and say—

sit down, friend, gee whiz, I can
see it in your eyes,

I can hear the sirens, blaring out
there in the dark
corners of your mind.
Please relax,

take a deep
breath, and

tell me: what
happened.

FIDDLE

The truth is
that art isn't
worth all that much.

The laundry is
far more important
than poetry;

a picture's 1000
word minimum
is short work for autofill.

But still,
there is something
beyond pleasure

in the slightest accord
between violin strings.
It's in the way

the whole thing shimmers
where its parts
made no difference,

or else strained
in imitation;
the way a lack

of explanation
satisfies our yearning
for inconsequence.

 A poem has no instructions,
but once read,
achieves summation

the way a baby's cry
means nothing, but delivers
consolation.

THE THINKING BRAIN

*Why do the phenomenon and its preconditions exist in the first place? Why not a different
mode of evolution not present on this planet that might have produced a different kind of
thinking brain?*
—Edward O. Wilson, *The Origins of Creativity*

Ingenious though it is,
the thinking brain
has the hardest time conceiving
of its opposite:
a simple star-shaped lump
of flesh
which moves around a lot
but doesn't
accomplish much.
To the mind,
the blind utility of muscle
is inconceivable.
And it's probably best
it remains so.
How we could come
to love one another
with just the prerequisite
of taking up space
is a hard enough
puzzle to solve as it is.
If we truly believed
these bodies were real,
we wouldn't want
anything to do with ourselves.

PRESTO CHANGE-O

What if
the Resurrection didn't
happen—presto
change-o—all at once?
What if this last
and best trick of all
was the gift
of open-ended process,
if this longest
of long shots was
still going on?
Think of that lesson:
all the little parochial kids
taught to love things
in increments,
not taught
to keep track, not
to count their blessings
only once
they've passed.

ALMOST SPRING POEM

Off the back
porch red railing, a
chip-toothed piano

keyboard of
old icicles dangling

unseen—except
by the sparrows; those
little bits

of lyrical
language about suffering—

thankfully
proclaiming: very little
outside

of their context.
Those things

which help us
suffer less—
we'll eventually have

to stop
abusing them too.

CULT CLASSIC

You know the one where you're
walking casually
down the street on an early
Sunday, and you see
the anointed ones—

the chosen few,
that narrow crowd
of purple tulips
wet with morning dew—

the strangeness
of those brainless creatures:
ethereal tubes that cannot move
and yet have found a way
of bending gently

but intently toward
the Sun, their great master
and silent teacher,

that cabalistic healer
who looks without seeing
and touches from afar,

that bizarre and monstrous
alien star, burning itself to
complete destruction
a billion times a billion
miles from here—

and for a moment you too
feel absolved,
released from your previous
angle of inclination,

humbled but exalted
by the braveness of color,

the stamina of these forms
of water, the pure white immensity
of light—

and all of a sudden
you find yourself
on board, transported
along with this blooming communion
of believers

to a place
where you're not
walking down the street anymore

but climbing
sideways
up the slope of a rock

so huge
and strange, it weighs
nothing?

FIRST PLACE

At the starting line, there are so often
things we mean to write or say
aphoristically—but it
never turns out that way.

In no time flat, the words begin
to clump in herds,
to yoke themselves up—and we
can't resist plowing

aimlessly forward:
mowing down the clean
mentality of trees,
uprooting the humbler mammals'

homes as we go on constructing
another eight lane road to god-
knows-where, without even caring
which direction we're going.

But then, where in hell have aphorisms
ever gotten us anyway?
I remember hearing once, for instance,
that love is all you need,

that it'd be just the thing
to light the way, to show us
where we were going and
where we would stay.

But now I think
the most useful emotion
is whichever one
is still in the tank,

whichever residual feeling
remains, whichever mood we still feel
lingering in the sweaty air
at the end of our labors

once we've finally had the courage
to drop every implement, turn
around filthy, and survey the truth
about where it is we came from.

54

INCORRUPTIBLE ACTUALITY

These measly fractions
of our lives—
the crumbs
we horde, shivering

and the theoretical
models of its atoms,
which we first have

to sketch,
then believe-in, then
remember—

they're such a small
part of it;
it's like we're all

staring—long and hard
at the world's
most precise

and sincere
and dazzlingly
beautiful mural,

one-eyed,
through a skinny
corroded length of pipe,

to witness one simple,
unsentimental
tile at a time.
This big picture—
if we could see it
mounted there

against the far wall
made of pure
white lightspeed—would be titled:
The Future is Only the Past Remembered

and the docent's little plaque
beside it
would probably read
something like:

The artist's intention here—was never
to win the war.
It was always, only, and ever
to end it.

OCCASIONAL POEM

With so much out of reach
now, I reach
for simplicity.

Don't want to say
any more
than I need to.

Don't need
to be Tolkien
to imagine: all's not lost.

Now is not the time
to weave
a complicated plot;

now is the time to ration
all the skillful
means I've got.

Only the melody
ought to get a solo;

only a splash
of Scotch for these rocks;

only the sharp keys
of short words

to pick the padlocks
on my big thoughts.

ALWAYS

Out of what must be millions
upon millions of those
maple tree whirlybirds,

my eye
always seems to focus
on one ruddy outlier

as it helicopters—
perilous, heroic,
and lonely—out and down

to some very likely inhospitable
patch of new ground.
And I wonder,

for the thousandth time:
whether
everything I am

is just all the things I can't
stop doing.
And then, for the first:

what will become
of that heap of leaves
if I keep neglecting to sweep it

since I always seem to be so busy
jotting-down these
spare phenomena?

INCONSEQUENT

From no practical instruction,
I have come to learn

that the June sun
around seven a.m.

is angled just right
for its light to become tangled,

momentarily fragmented
and trapped

in the tightly weaved branches
of two sweetgum trees

at the end of my street, just such
that I can linger beneath

and freely observe it
fixed there: halcyon, pacific;

as if standing—like god would,
like the word did

in the beginning
before it could be spoken

or heard—completely implicit,
inconsequent of time.

That I am there promptly
each morning

to see it—makes no difference;
that I am here now

to say it—matters
every little bit.

CHRIST

Christ, if I
could just bring

some water
to those workers

struggling on the pavement—
you know the ones—

hardhatted, neonvested,
rippling in the distant sun—

that would be
the simplest thing

the purest thing
the only thing—

clear wet water
in little white cups—

the most transparent
thing I've ever done.

WHY I WRITE, MK. II

Because I love to talk—
to give ethereal form
to thoughts

but can't stand the sound
of the yowling
whelps that come out.

Because I once was lost
and embarrassed
to get directions

but now I'm found
and too proud
to acknowledge it.

Because I can never get enough
of the great void opened up
by repetition

but I'm terrified
of that silence which lurks
inside silence.

Because I have
an avian soul—the itinerant brain
of a bird

but the four-
chambered heart
of a nervous old birdwatcher.

Because—how good
are those rare gifted songbirds
we take time to notice,

but how much better
must be all those
we miss?

MANIFEST

At the center
of how
you always

try to pin things
down

is a nucleus
made out of
reasons why

you mostly succeed
in screwing them up.

Imagine
the scalded
cauldron of your grief

without that name
you gave it;

picture delineating
the difference
between

professional
and amateur nobodies;

close your eyes
and see if you
can imitate

the legible melody
your soul would sing

without
all the notes
it doesn't need.

THE ROAD NOT RETAKEN

I took the one less traveled by,
And that has made all the difference.
—Robert Frost

Actually, after Frost did
or did not get lost,
the road not taken
didn't stay open much longer.
Somewhere downtown,

in a marble building's basement,
it was sold for a song,
bulldozed to pieces,
regraded, repaved, covered-
over like a skin lesion.

There's a better-lit bus stop
and a closer-by grocery store
and a high-rise retirement
condominium's auxiliary pick-up
and drop-off lot there now—

and a few people are sad about this
inexorable honing of our
decision-making process, and several
more are happy about it, and the rest
still can't work out the difference.

TOUCH ME NOT

Red impatiens,
white impatiens,
pink impatiens,
yellow—dilating

in an obscured
sort of row

on the easement
adjacent to this
fraught intersection—oh

how I adore
that no one asks
what's best for you;

they've just left you alone
to do the one
thing you

already know
how to do.

OH SNAIL

O snail
Climb Mount Fuji
But slowly, slowly!
—Issa (trans. R.H. Blyth)

Slow and steady
wins the race, I guess
but what if the
race isn't real? No slope,
no sky, it's all
a shell we live inside
as a dreamer
whose vulnerable
mind secretes, in defense,
a fortifying dream.
Will it ever be possible
to succeed
at such a climb—or
to fail? And how
could you tell
the difference? Oh snail,
what the hell?

AFTER THE POEM IS DONE

Of the tens of murky self-
similar thousands,
there is only one

crystalline moment
immediately after
the poem is done

in which I don't feel exceptional
pressure to explain
anything to anyone;

not the intimate
nature of my relationship
to friction and its coefficients,

not the gory details
of my long-standing three-way
with Gravity and the Normal Force,

not even the vague way in which
uselessness wells up and
clashes with hope

when I stop to acknowledge
the velocity at which
the surface of the earth has been rotating.

For one rock-solid second,
I feel obligated
never to explain

anything that's been going on with me
ever again.
And when this happens,

it's such a strange combination
of a relief
and a rush,

a hybridized feeling
so complete, yet unique—
almost to the point

of being unheard-of—that
just this once, I
had to tell someone.

67

EXCHANGE

I hereby pledge,
every day, to make you
fresh music

using the only two
means that I've got:

those syllables of English
speech which are
stressed,

and those
which are not.

I'll arrange these
small words into
glimmering patterns—

based on the ones
I first learned
(before I knew

how to put on a raincoat
or tie my own shoes)
by memorizing,

then parroting back
the glimmering
fuss of grown-ups.

But in exchange
for all that, I want you
to promise

to take precious care
of my instruments:

the measure
and pitch of the voice
in your head

and the moment-
to-moment endurance
of your breath.

69

MINUS THE DYNAMITE

Recall
the last time you
felt the warm weight

of a nickel
in your hand

and honestly
thought you might
purchase something with it.

Imagine being presented
with a granny smith apple
as a Christmas present

by someone
who really meant it.

The short poem is like that.
It's an angel—
not a real one

(the kind a desperate
person may need
to believe in),

but one of those
white plaster quarter-size
statues of one:

not so great to look at—
and minus the dynamite
singing voice—

but at least
it can neither vanish

nor inspire
any hate.

THE FLOWERS OF NONCHALANCE

It used to
make me feel
like a deity

to smash
the occasional hairy
brown spider

scuttling
down the length
of my hallway molding—

the way I'd swoop down
from outside
its ontology,

as if forcefully teaching
its whole phylum
a lesson.

But gradually,
it's begun to make me feel
like a casualty

to always be teaching,
never learning
from these sessions.

I've thought—could it be
even more radical still
to pivot and turn

on that retributive foot?
To tend, if not
to the gardens of mercy,

than at least
to the flowers
of nonchalance?

Can I yet learn to do
that which
daunts me most

and spurn a god
who must manifest
his worth?

And will
learning to do so
somehow make me

omnipotent
right here on earth?

SILENCE SPEAKS

Listen:
just underneath
the clamor

of the Earth
as she's heaving

her second-
to-last breath;

just in-between
our having come this far
reluctantly

and the chaotic way
we are cleft
as we leave—

an absence
interposes;

a silence
that speaks.

There are moments, it says,
when we can't act
as we must;

there are endings
far more everlasting
than heaven—

yet less abrupt
than death.

WORLD OF DEW

You don't know
a lot,

but you think
it's safe to assume
that

all things
are desperate—

to open up
and show you
what they've got.

You suspect—
there are
all kinds of feelings

you finally might
meet the words for
soon.

Last night,
you could
see the shiny

milk white
quarter moon,

ringed
with tiny
forever stars

and cradling
the ghost

of the full moon
in its spindly arms,
and felt

willing to bet—
someone
or something

was
trying to forget

everything
that has
ever happened,

and, in the process,
apprehending
something

really big
that hasn't yet.

A POET

is hardly an author
the way a maker
of forests is—

a black squirrel, spitting acorns,
a brown finch,
shedding seeds.

Then again:
it's a relative cinch,

to grow something complex
as an oak tree

from a blueprint
or sketch—

but it's hell
collapsing it back
to the acorn again.

FOR EMILY

To the poet, is possibility
really so much fairer
a house in which to dwell
than prose?

The abstract made tangible
seems a double-edged sword—
to be liberated, at length,
is to find yourself unmoored

in a closet-
sized hell
where defining
spells confinement

and the devil presiding grows
bored of the details—but never
the impregnable strength
of your rhyming.

SANCTUARY

While it rains
and rains,
putting the alley sparrows

and the cardinal
who sings
in the park out of work,

I am grateful
to be employed at all—

let alone so gainfully
building a vast new city
of expressivity—

or at least
a whole district
of rhetorical churches—

or at least a neat
row of simple
dwellings made of words—

or at least adequate shelving
in the dry narrow galley
kitchen of my mind

for those aforementioned
birds to perch on.

MIXED FEELINGS

You keep hearing—
the gray light of sunrise
is far and away the very
best kind of light. But you'll

never be able to say it
like that. For that matter,
what was it the fog rolling
in off lake Michigan

was trying to call out to you
this morning? What on earth
did the black coffee afterward
actually taste like?

So many things
you'll never be able to tell
that have to be told anyway.
It's just business is usually

how the businessmen put it.
This is the province of science
claims a dental hygienist.
But the poet says—maybe

this is just how it is. Maybe
you only have mixed feelings
about everything
because there's no such thing

as a pure one.
All you can say is—I love this
too, and wait around
for the emptiness (which

chokes closed the last
line of every poem)
to rush in and confabulate
the rest of the details. Maybe it's

pure selfishness
which first drove the mute
soul to dream. Maybe
each new story that's told

is only there to help us
make sense of our own.
Maybe the stars are fading
because it's finally morning.

80

LIKENESS

By the time it's
all over,
instead of a story,

I hope that my life
presents more
like a painting—

brazen and wide,
and hung right
at eye-level,

so that everyone who enters
cannot help
but regard it—

but no one
may come

to say for certain
what I've done—

only to see
the totality

of me
having done it
all at once.

UNRUNG BELL

O tacit metal;
o infinite odds;
o fire without color, heat,
brightness, or smell;

o shapely goddess
of fictive music—
I hope you never tell
us a hint of the riddle.

Disregard this, as you dispel
all that trembles.
If you're still
listening—don't even nod.

Grateful acknowledgements are due to the editors of the following publications in which some of these poems first appeared:

The Blue Mountain Review, "What Happened"
Jabberwock Review, "What's One More"
The Los Angeles Review, "Incorruptible Actuality"
The Ocotillo Review, "Fiddle," "Le Mot Juste," "Silence Speaks"

84